To Marcia - Than.. f..
..wing us such a gl..
Rotary International 2005..

Pat Davidson } Bracebridge
Bill Nodwell } Ontario
                Canada.

W9-AGM-102

The Little Gift Book of
ONTARIO

The Little Gift Book of

ONTARIO

Whitecap Books
Vancouver/Toronto

Copyright © 1991 by Whitecap Books
Whitecap Books
Vancouver/Toronto

Text by Darby Macnab
Edited by Linda Ostrowalker
Cover and Interior design by Doug Smith
Typography by CompuType, Vancouver, B.C., Canada

Printed and bound in Canada by Friesen Printers,
   Altona, Manitoba

Canadian Cataloguing in Publication Data
   Macnab, Darby.
      The little gift book of Ontario

   ISBN 1-895099-88-9

   1. Ontario—Description and travel—1981—Views. I. Title.
FC3067.5.M32 1991   971.3'04'0222   C91-091471-0
F1057.M32 1991

Cover: Idyllic cottages in the Thousand Islands. *Gera Dillon/First Light*

Contents

The Gardiner Expressway looking towards downtown Toronto.

Ontario

Ontario is an Iroquois word meaning "shining waters"—an appropriate name for a province bordered in the southwest by four of the Great Lakes, in the north by Hudson and James Bay, and interspersed throughout with myriad lakes and rivers. It was these waterways that led the earliest native inhabitants to the riches of the interior—the forests, wildlife, and minerals that sustained them. Later, European explorers would ply these same rivers and lakes, travelling ever deeper into the continent, initially seeking a passage east, but later intent on fur trading and settling the land.

In the early years of British and French empire-building, many native tribes fared well. Furs were traded for European goods as the Hudson's Bay Company established posts throughout the territory, and Jesuits preached Christianity while learning wilderness survival techniques from their na-

Sheltered moorings at Oakville, just west
of Toronto on Lake Ontario.

tive converts. Throughout the eighteenth century disease and warfare devastated native populations and, as territorial struggles between Britain and France escalated, many tribes gave up their land.

Britain claimed territorial victory over France in 1759, and twenty years later the American Revolution sent thousands of pro-British immigrants north to present-day Ontario. Soon afterwards, Upper and Lower Canada were divided by the same border that exists between Quebec and Ontario today.

Upper Canada soon became the hub of English-speaking Canada. Its central location on what was to become the Great Lakes-St. Lawrence Seaway gave access to world markets, and the abundant resources of the surrounding land fuelled trade and industry. Then, as now, the region's many assets attracted huge numbers of immigrants.

Little wonder that Ontario is now Canada's most populous and prosperous province. The fertile south abounds with productive farmlands, while the Golden Horseshoe area on the shores of Lake Ontario is the manufacturing and industrial core of the province. The many lakes of central Ontario offer an accessible summer haven for cottagers and outdoor enthusiasts, while the north, dotted with small towns and communities, still contains vast expanses of untainted wilderness. Some of Canada's greatest wealth comes from the minerals found in the ancient rocks of the Canadian Shield — nickel, copper, silver, gold, platinum, cobalt, and uranium — while forestry and hydroelectric power are also major economic mainstays.

From the subarctic, barren wilderness of Hudson Bay's shores to the balmy, fruit-growing regions of the Niagara Peninsula; from the monuments and heritage sites of its oldest settlements to the timeless beauty of the land north of Lake Superior; from the thrum of urban centres to the call of a loon on a sparkling northern lake, Ontario's landscapes are as diverse as its people.

Lily pads in a tranquil lake in Muskoka.

Toronto

When John Graves Simcoe, the first governor of Upper Canada, founded the town of York in 1793, little did he know that it would become the mighty city that is Toronto today. A sprawling metropolis of over 3 million people, Toronto is the financial nerve-centre of the country, and a showcase of fine architecture and city planning; a safe, clean, attractive city that features world-class hospitality and cuisine, a flourishing arts community, and a widely divergent cultural mix.

Old York has come a long way from its staid, British-loyalist origins. Its early prosperity was based on farming, but emigrating merchants, tradesmen, and labourers soon created a healthy trade and manufacturing sector on the shores of Lake Ontario. By 1834, when the town was renamed Toronto (a Mississauga Indian word meaning "meeting place"), there were about nine thousand residents and it was well on its way to becoming the hub of English-speaking Canada.

Evening rush hour on the 401 highway in Toronto.

While its early history was dominated by the British, waves of immigrants from all over the world have settled in Toronto over this century, creating a tapestry of thriving international communities. Encouraged to keep their individual cultures alive, each community maintains a presence within the city through its shops, markets, religious institutions, and cultural centres. Cohesive neighbourhoods of Chinese, Italians, East Asians, Europeans, Africans, and many others, give Toronto a rich, cosmopolitan texture. Through the shops of Chinatown (one of North America's largest), the East Indian restaurants, the Italian cafés, the Portuguese fish markets, the flamboyant Caribbean "Caribana" festival, or the stunning beauty of the Japanese Cultural Centre, one can virtually tour the cultures of the world within the bounds of Metropolitan Toronto.

Toronto's role as Canada's financial capital was established early in this century, and this affluence is reflected in its architecture. Downtown, a phalanx of glass and steel towers stand as monuments to national corporations and financial institutions, while SkyDome's retractable roof and the CN Tower's 1815-foot spire create an unmistakably unique skyline.

In the shadows of these modern structures stand many gracious old buildings, such as St. James' Cathedral, dating from 1853, and the Provincial Legislature at Queen's Park Circle, built in 1886.

Fifty years of careful city planning has resulted in Toronto becoming a very "liveable" city. Its well-maintained downtown core is dotted with green areas, while the sprawling, picturesque acreage of large parks such as High Park or Edward's Gardens offer great recreational opportunities. Toronto's many theatres, restaurants, clubs, galleries, museums, and professional sports teams provide a heady mix of activities for residents and visitors alike.

A Toronto Island ferry approaches its berth in the early evening.

Pedestrians at lunch hour downtown.

Osgoode Hall with Old City Hall beyond.

Victorian semi-detached homes in the historic
Kensington Market neighbourhood.

*Shovelling snow after a winter storm in
the heart of downtown.*

*The Manufacturer's Life Building
on Bloor Street East.*

*The fabled flatiron building
between Front and Wellington streets.*

The Provincial Legislature Building
at Queen's Park.

*The curving towers of Toronto's
City Hall at dusk.*

*Toronto's Centre Island is a short
15-minute ferry ride from downtown.*

*The affluent Rosedale neighbourhood
is steps away from downtown.*

Toronto's Centre Island in winter.

*Dundas Street West is home to
a vibrant and lively Chinatown.*

*Roncesvalles Avenue is the heart
of the Polish district.*

Fresh fruit for sale in Chinatown.

*Casa Loma, Toronto's only genuine
castle, built in 1911 by
Sir Henry Pellatt.*

*Skydome, sold out as usual
for a Toronto Blue Jays game.*

Two of Toronto's greatest modern architectural marvels, Skydome and the CN Tower.

*Children gaze at one of the exhibits
at the world-famous Science Centre.*

Southwestern Ontario

Ontario's southwest corner, wedged in by Lakes Huron, Erie, and Ontario, holds some of the province's finest farmland — as well as the bustling and populous urban sprawl known as the Golden Horseshoe. Stretching around Lake Ontario's western end, this is the industrial and manufacturing core of the province. From Oshawa, home to General Motors of Canada, through Toronto, and around to Hamilton, the country's steel-producing capital, its residents make up nearly half the province's population.

The nearby Niagara Peninsula, jutting between Lakes Erie and Ontario, enjoys ideal fruit-growing conditions. Balmy summer days and fertile soil support bounteous orchards and vineyards, the latter sustaining a healthy wine-growing industry. Tourists flocking to this picturesque region are drawn to the beautifully preserved nineteenth-century town of Niagara-on-the-Lake. Sitting on Lake Ontario at the American border, this is the home of the annual Shaw Theatre festival. Originally called Newark, it was the first capi-

The Ambassador Bridge links Windsor with the more northerly city of Detroit, Michigan.

tal of Upper Canada, and was burned down during the War of 1812. Nearby, a towering monument stands in commemoration of British General Sir Isaac Brock's heroic death at the battle of Queenston Heights. Another prominent wartime Canadian was Laura Secord, who travelled thirty kilometres overnight to warn British troops of an imminent American attack. Her homestead, authentically restored to the turn-of-the-century period, is also found here. Just south along the Niagara River thunders one of the world's natural wonders — Niagara Falls. More than 150 million litres of water catapult over the horseshoe-shaped falls every minute in this dramatic presentation of nature's power.

Further west stands the town of Brantford, named after the famous Mohawk, Captain Joseph Brant, who, with his people, sided with Britain against France during the eighteenth-century territorial struggles here. Brantford remains today an important Mohawk cultural centre and reserve.

Closer to Lake Huron lie rolling farmlands, yielding forage crops, mixed grains, corn, and barley, which sustain hog, dairy, and beefstock farms throughout the region. The Kitchener-Waterloo area is home to a large Mennonite community — a European sect whose time-honoured ways of life include farming their enormously prosperous land by horsepower alone. Other early settlers to this area were of German origin. Their Oktoberfest festival, held every fall, has become the largest of its kind in North America. Over 600,000 people come each year to enjoy the finest in Bavarian sausage, sauerkraut, and oompah music. Nearby, the Stratford Festival has become a world-class annual theatre event.

Ontario's — and, in fact, Canada's — southernmost point juts out into Lake Erie at Point Pelee, a small peninsula on the same latitude as northern California. This national park abounds with grass, trees, marshlands, and beaches, and is a popular resting spot for migrating birds — and avid bird-watchers.

Stratford-on-Avon, home of the renowned
Shakespeare Theatre Festival.

An aerial view of Canada's Horseshoe Falls at Niagara Falls.

Main Street in Drayton in autumn.

*One of the many prosperous farms
in rural Ontario.*

*The U.S./Canadian border is formed by
the Niagara River at Niagara Falls.*

Sunrise in a corn field near Mitchell.

St. Mark's Parish Hall,
Niagara-on-the-Lake.

Rich agricultural land near Fonthill.

*A friendly horse looks over a typical
wooden fence at Black Creek Pioneer
Village.*

*Concorde grapes ready for the harvest
near Grimsby.*

The marsh boardwalk at Point Pelee
National Park is a birdwatcher's
paradise.

Southeastern Ontario

To the east of Metropolitan Toronto, the urban sprawl gives way to gentler country. Along the shores of Lake Ontario lie fertile agricultural lands dotted with small towns rich in history. Near Picton the shoreline rises in astonishing sand dunes reaching thirty metres in height, while to the north, lakelands and rocky highlands rise to meet the edge of the Canadian Shield.

The southeastern corner of Ontario is part of Canada's historical heartland. Towns and communities here reverberate with the culture and heritage of those who settled them — the homesteaders, lumbermen, and miners who were originally attracted to the land's rich resources. Many of the United Empire Loyalists who emigrated to Canada after the American Revolution in 1776 came to the Ottawa Valley and the northern shores of the St. Lawrence, and their influence is reflected in the church spires, cemeteries, and period buildings that remain.

Where Lake Ontario flows into the mighty St. Lawrence River lies the

A rear view of the towers of
Parliament Hill in Ottawa.

43

town of Kingston. Once the capital of the United Provinces of Canada, its classical city hall dating from 1844, as well as many other distinctive period buildings, make it a showcase of colonial heritage. Nearby stands Fort Henry, the restored nineteenth-century fortress that was once Upper Canada's principal stronghold. To the east, between Gananoque and Brockville, lie the Thousand Islands, a popular resort area of distinctive natural beauty.

From Kingston northeast to Ottawa runs the famous Rideau Canal, built for military purposes after the War of 1812. Now entirely given over to recreation, this gentle waterway passes through the small towns and communities of the Ottawa Valley and the Rideau Lakes region. The town that originally developed around the canal's excavation site on the Ottawa River was known as Bytown, and quickly became the hub of the Ottawa Valley's burgeoning lumber trade in the early nineteenth century. By 1855, it had changed its name to Ottawa, and in 1867, Queen Victoria herself selected it as the capital of the newly confederated Dominion of Canada.

Ottawa, together with the city of Hull on Quebec's side of the border, functions as the National Capital Region. Ottawa has grown into a cosmopolitan city, replete with fabulous parks, gardens, and impressive architecture, while Hull embodies the French element of the national capital. Parliament Hill, Canada's seat of government, stands high atop the bluffs overlooking the Ottawa River. Its gracious, copper-roofed gothic buildings serve as the city's nucleus, while myriad museums, historical residences, and public buildings are to be found nearby.

*Skaters jam the Rideau Canal during
Ottawa's "Winterlude."*

Crowds throng Sparks Street in Ottawa.

The peaceful Rideau Canal in Ottawa's summer sunshine.

Bolt Castle in the Thousand Islands area of the St. Lawrence River.

Cadets in eighteenth-century uniforms enact the evening ceremony at Fort Henry in Kingston.

A shopkeeper waits for trade at
Upper Canada Village in Morrisburg.

Holy Trinity Anglican Church
at Shawmasville.

Summer sunset at a farm near Bowmanville.

*Sand Dunes Provincial Park in Prince
Edward County on Lake Ontario.*

The Lakelands

From farmlands, marshes, and the sparkling Kawartha Lakes in the east, to the deep, cool lakes and rocky isles of Muskoka, and the vast stretches of sandy beaches at Georgian Bay, this is cottage and resort country at its finest.

Through the heart of Ontario's lakelands region winds the Trent-Severn Waterway, beginning at Trenton on Lake Ontario and emerging at Georgian Bay on Lake Huron. Originally the route taken by Samuel de Champlain in 1615, this series of lakes and rivers was linked by locks and canals to service the booming economy of nineteenth-century Ontario. Today, only pleasure craft travel the 384-kilometre route, aided by some impressive technology, from The Big Chute Marine Railway, which carries boats past a difficult section of the Severn River, to the world's highest (20-metre) hydraulic lift lock at Peterborough.

Long before the first Europeans made their way through these lakes and

Hardy Lake Provincial Park in Muskoka.

rivers, native tribes reigned supreme, living off nature's abundant supplies. Early seventeenth-century records report Hurons living in the Georgian Bay area, while the Algonquin tribes lived to the south throughout what is now Muskoka. A nomadic people, the Algonquin traded regularly with the Huron, exchanging furs and hides for agricultural products from Huron farms.

It was near present-day Midland, on the shores of Georgian Bay, that the first Jesuit mission — Sainte-Marie Among the Hurons — was established in 1639. For the next ten years, the Jesuits preached Christianity, while the Huron taught them how to survive in the wilderness. During this time, disease ran rampant through the native population and their numbers were greatly reduced, but it was Iroquois raids which brought about their final demise. Surprise attacks, plus the capture and torture of several Jesuit priests eventually caused survivors to burn the mission and flee, thus ending the region's first inland European settlement.

To the west juts the Bruce Peninsula, part of the rocky spine that stretches between Lake Ontario and Manitoulin Island. This is Ontario's newest national park, featuring some of the Niagara Escarpment's most spectacular scenery. The waters off the tip of the peninsula are legendary for their many shipwrecks, and divers flock here to investigate this underwater history in the clear, cold waters of Georgian Bay. From Tobermory, ferries leave for Manitoulin Island, the world's largest freshwater island, featuring long, sandy beaches and age-old towns and villages.

*The big flower pot on Flower Pot Island in
the Georgian Bay Islands National Park.*

Busy Beaumaris Marina in Muskoka.

*Rocking chairs wait invitingly at sunrise
in Cottage Country.*

*Sunrise over the fertile Holland Marsh
just north of Toronto.*

*Morning fog lingers over an onion field
near Holland Marsh.*

The historic steamship "Seguin" at
her mooring at Gravenhurst.

A tranquil canoe scene in northern Ontario.

Evening colours at dusk in Muskoka.

Large barns, such as this one near Durham, are found throughout Ontario.

The Near North

A windswept white pine, a stand of hard maples, the grey face of the Canadian Shield, a sparkling northern lake — these images, made famous by the Canadian Group of Seven painters, were inspired by the natural beauty of Ontario's near north. From the eastern shore of Lake Superior to Algonquin Park, the wilderness areas have taken on an almost mystical quality. Much of the landscape remains unchanged since French explorers first marvelled at it over three hundred years ago.

In the seventeenth century, the lakes and rivers of central Ontario led the French-Canadian voyageurs ever northwards, and their legacy remains; monuments to Etienne Brûlé and Samuel de Champlain at North Bay, the bilingual Laurentian University in Sudbury, and, of course, Sault Ste. Marie — an ancient native meeting place at the junction of Lakes Huron and Superior settled by French missionaries in the late seventeenth century. It later developed into a major fur trading post for the Hudson's Bay and

Fall colours in Algonquin Park.

North West companies.

"The Soo," as it is called, sitting across the St. Mary's River from its American counterpart, Sault Ste. Marie, Michigan, saw plenty of action during the War of 1812. British forces were aided by Indian allies in their cross-border raids while, in 1814, the Canadian settlement was destroyed by the Americans. Just after this, a fur trading baron named Ermating built a stone house that still stands today — the oldest structure of its kind in northern Ontario. Today, Sault Ste. Marie is a major steel producing centre boasting one of the most active canals in the entire St. Lawrence Seaway system. Meanwhile, the nearby Agawa Canyon is an ever-present reminder of the grandeur of nature; its dark forests, dramatic waterfalls, gorges, and fjord-like ravines show the northern landscape at its finest.

In sharp contrast to this scenic splendour lies the Sudbury Basin to the southeast. Believed to have been formed by a meteorite crash, the flattened landscape here is positively lunar, but beneath it lies the fabulous mineral wealth that has made the town of Sudbury the nickel capital of the world. Also found here are large stores of cobalt, copper, gold, and platinum. Sudbury is also home to Science North — an impressive science museum featuring hands-on physics, biology, and geology exhibits.

To the east, not far from the Quebec border, lies the legendary Algonquin Provincial Park. Established in 1893, its 7600 square kilometres of lakes, rivers, and forests have been carefully preserved. With only one road cutting through the park, it is a paradise for hikers and canoeists, who share the wilds with moose, deer, bears, beavers, wolves, and many other creatures typical of the Canadian Shield.

*A canoeist explores Cache Lake
in Algonquin Park.*

Log cabins and stump fences such as these used to be found all over rural Ontario.

*Setting off for a winter camp
in Algonquin Park.*

*The best way to explore Algonquin Park
is by canoe.*

*The famed Canada Goose statue
at Wawa.*

*The International Bridge and Canal locks
at Sault Ste. Marie.*

An aerial view of downtown Sudbury looking towards the lake.

*A typical scene in the Temagami region
of northern Ontario.*

*The bright sails on these dinghies provide a
splash of colour on a lake in Algonquin Park.*

The Northern Wilderness

The land north of Lake Superior is stunningly beautiful — a forested wilderness interspersed with pristine lakes fed by rivers that course south into Lake Superior, or north towards Hudson Bay. A series of thriving, friendly communities cling to the north shore of Superior — the largest fresh-water lake in the world — while to the north, towns, and even roads, are rare. Remote communities north of here rely on the fly-in services, as do the area's many world-class hunting and fishing lodges.

Long before the French Canadian voyageurs reached these northern shores, Sioux and Ojibwa tribes battled over the land so rich in wildlife, forests, minerals, and fresh water. Mining and forestry have been economic mainstays of this region since its earliest days. Almost every community has a mine, or a lumber mill, or a pulp and paper mill. Nipigon, once home

Blowing snow in winter obscures the Lake Superior shore.

79

to the Ojibwa, was the first white settlement on the north shore of Lake Superior. Strategically located at the mouth of the Nipigon River, it was a thriving fur trading centre before Fort William became the headquarters of the North West Company. Fort William's Great Rendezvous became an annual event where over one thousand trappers, traders, natives, and adventurers met each summer to trade beaver pelts for blankets and alcohol. Fort William has been reconstructed as it stood in 1815, a fascinating window into the region's colourful past.

Thunder Bay has replaced Fort William as the hub of the north shore. This bustling, multi-cultural centre boasts Canada's third largest port and an international airport. The towering waterside elevators reflect the huge amounts of grain that pass through here from the Prairies to world markets via the St. Lawrence Seaway. The Lake of the Woods region lies to the northwest — an idyllic labyrinth of bays, islets, and inlets that has long been a recreation and resort destination.

Far to the north of Ontario's populous core lie great expanses of wilderness where moose, deer, bears, and wolves run free. The characteristic rock of the Canadian Shield dominates the landscape, offering up mineral riches and creating a rough-hewn beauty.

One of the Hudson's Bay Company's oldest trading posts was located at Moose Factory, established in 1673 at the mouth of the Moose River. Today's explorers can board the Polar Bear Express and ride 300 kilometres through forest and muskeg to Moosonee, where Cree Indians offer canoe trips to Moose Factory and a glimpse into the past at the Cree Cultural Centre.

Most of the communities that dot the northern landscape follow the line of the Canadian National Railway and are the sites of fantastic mineral wealth. In 1903, one of the world's richest veins of silver gave rise to the town of Cobalt, while gold put Timmins and Kirkland Lake on the map. Kapuskasing (the "Kleenex Capital") and Iroquois Falls are pulp and paper towns.

Stretches of untouched wilderness abound: dense forests of spruce, aspen, and jack pine are interrupted only by the sound of rushing water, or the call of a loon on a silent lake. Sportsmen flock here to take advantage of some of the world's finest hunting and fishing, while others come simply to enjoy the serenity of the wild, breathtaking scenery. Superb recreational opportunities can be found in provincial parks such as Polar Bear Provincial Park which, standing on the shores of Hudson Bay, is accessible only by plane.

An aerial view of Ouimet Canyon Provincial
Park north of Lake Superior.

*Grain elevators reflected in the calm waters
of Lake Superior at Thunder Bay.*

Pie Island in the distance near
Thunder Bay.

*The Common Loon is to be found on
lakes throughout Ontario.*

*The island-studded Kam River near
Lake Superior.*

The small town of Webequie is almost
surrounded by water.

*Polar bears are residents of the
James Bay frontier.*

Fresh snow falls on a quiet northern scene.

*The church at Upsala seems to grow
out of a field of daisies.*

Photo Credits

Paul von Baich/First Light p. 45
Grant Black/First Light pp. 78, 88
Michael E. Burch pp. 1, 11, 14, 16, 19, 24, 37, 39, 42, 51
Mark Burnham/First Light p. 34
J. Cochrane/First Light pp. 46, 47
Gera Dillon/First Light pp. iii, 12, 28, 70
Barry Dursley/First Light pp. 5, 54, 58, 64
Janet Dwyer/First Light pp. 36, 40
First Light Toronto pp. 33, 61
Dawn Goss/First Light p. 38
David Prichard Kingston/First Light p. 49
Thomas Kitchin/First Light pp. 10, 18, 35, 73, 74, 75, 81, 82, 85
Jerry Kobalenko/First Light p. 86
Todd Korol/First Light p. 65
Robert Lankinen/First Light pp. 84, 87
Greg Locke/First Light p. 63
Mary Ellen McQuay/First Light p. 52
M. P. Manheim/First Light p. 17
Brian Milne/First Light pp. 15, 20, 83, 89
Jessie Parker/First Light pp. 48, 50
Lorraine C. Parow/First Light pp. 22, 31
Dave Prichard/First Light p. 66
Jim Russell/First Light p. 25
A. E. Sirulnikoff/First Light p. 23
Donald Stanfield/First Light pp. 59, 71, 72, 76, 77
Ken Straiton/First Light pp. 2, 21, 53, 62
Ron Watts/First Light pp. 6, 9, 13, 26, 27, 32, 60, 69
Wayne Wegner/First Light pp. 41, 57